To Angela —

with love.

Ellye.

HOW TO
FIND YOUR
INNER HAPPINESS

MY JOURNEY

E R CLARIDGE

BALBOA
PRESS
A DIVISION OF HAY HOUSE

Copyright © 2017 E R Claridge.

All rights reserved. No part of this book may be used or reproduced by any means, graphic, electronic, or mechanical, including photocopying, recording, taping or by any information storage retrieval system without the written permission of the author except in the case of brief quotations embodied in critical articles and reviews.

Balboa Press books may be ordered through booksellers or by contacting:

Balboa Press
A Division of Hay House
1663 Liberty Drive
Bloomington, IN 47403
www.balboapress.com
1 (877) 407-4847

Because of the dynamic nature of the Internet, any web addresses or links contained in this book may have changed since publication and may no longer be valid. The views expressed in this work are solely those of the author and do not necessarily reflect the views of the publisher, and the publisher hereby disclaims any responsibility for them.

The author of this book does not dispense medical advice or prescribe the use of any technique as a form of treatment for physical, emotional, or medical problems without the advice of a physician, either directly or indirectly. The intent of the author is only to offer information of a general nature to help you in your quest for emotional and spiritual well-being. In the event you use any of the information in this book for yourself, which is your constitutional right, the author and the publisher assume no responsibility for your actions.

Any people depicted in stock imagery provided by Thinkstock are models, and such images are being used for illustrative purposes only. Certain stock imagery © Thinkstock.

Print information available on the last page.

ISBN: 978-1-5043-6759-2 (sc)
ISBN: 978-1-5043-6760-8 (e)

Balboa Press rev. date: 01/16/2017

CONTENTS

Introduction ix

Chapter One - How it started 1

Chapter Two - Peoples fear and insecurities drain our energy 7

Chapter Three - A big down fall is Jealousy 13

Chapter Four - What do you feel? 19

Chapter Five - How did it affect me? 21

Chapter Six - Another case 27

Chapter Seven - What is an intention and influence? ... 29

Chapter Eight - So what's it all about how do we get in this mentally confused state? 34

Chapter Nine - What is Energy and how does it affect us? 37

Chapter Ten - How do outside influences change our energy? 39

Chapter Eleven - How does gossip affect our vibrations? 42

Chapter Twelve - The power of music 46

Chapter Thirteen - The brain 49

Chapter Fourteen - Electrical Impulses on the Brain 51

Chapter Fifteen - Neurotransmitters 54

Chapter Sixteen - Pineal Gland 57

Chapter Seventeen - Mental Health 59

Chapter Eighteen - High Vibration 62

Chapter Nineteen - The Signs 64

Chapter Twenty - The Conclusion 69

References 73

Bibliography 75

An Old Cherokee Tale of Two Wolves

One evening an old Cherokee Indian told his grandson about a battle that goes on inside people. He said, 'My son, the battle is between two 'wolves' inside us all. One is Evil. It is anger, envy, jealousy, sorrow, regret, greed, arrogance, self-pity, guilt, resentment, inferiority, lies, false pride, superiority, and ego.

The other is good. It is joy, peace, love, hope, serenity, humility, kindness, benevolence, empathy, generosity, truth, compassion and faith.'

The grandson thought about it for a minute and then asked his grandfather: 'Which wolf wins?'

The old Cherokee simply replied, 'The one you feed.'

INTRODUCTION

THERE ARE NO explanations in this world that tells us why things happen as they do. The only thing I am being shown now is how important and strong the LOVE energy is.

When we fall the victim to other people fear, this can so easily block us mentally and physically. As the energies our body are carrying have been contaminated with other energies, and our body calls out to reject this by ill health, both physically and mentally.

Through my own experiences, I hope to make people aware how low vibrations contaminate us and how we can clear these low vibrations (others fears) so we can embrace the right journey. Through embracing our passions and positive energies into our life we can carry on a happy and bountiful life. When we are carrying low vibrations, it's very difficult to distinguish what is good for us and what isn't. When we are contaminated the law of attraction, will attract the same. If you carry negative energy, you will attract negative energy.

Chapter One

HOW IT STARTED

MY AWAKENING STARTED back in 2010, when everything and everyone I loved in my life wasn't in a good place. I felt like I had this invisible wall blocking me everywhere I turned. I didn't know what I wanted anymore as I couldn't distinguish what made me happy.

I felt confused and felt like my mind was taking on a new current of its own, nothing made sense and I was searching for something that would make me realise what it was all about.

At the time I was very concerned for my friend's health as she struggling, and it was scary times. There were several occasions when anything she was ate or drank made her ill. Prescription drugs made her ill so we knew it was very difficult to seek medical advice.

It was one emotional roller coaster after another as nothing was making sense; how one day she could have a good day and eat more, and then another day it was back to where we started.

There was one thing that just made me realise there is more to life than we see. I thought there has got to be another way, my gut instinct told me it wasn't just my friends ill health. As she ate healthy, didn't drink, didn't smoke, she was extremely healthy in other ways, and a very positive person. This really didn't make sense.

My intuition started to become heightened and stronger, I started to recall messages in my dreams and early morning I would get these inner feelings, it was like an awakening to what the universe was telling me. I really started to listen to my gut instinct and acted on it. To the point the next time she had a nasty attack, I laid my hands on her stomach and asked for her pain to be transferred to me, it worked. She felt stronger and recovered from the attack much quicker. I on the other hand felt so tired, and had an uncomfortable stomach. I could take a stomach settler, so we got by that way.

However something clicked, this was an exchange of energy that had taken place, and my gut instinct was right, there was more to this!

I started to feel drawn to natural tools like the earth's natural stones, all different types of crystals, and I started to work with them. I would feel drawn to different stones at different stages in my life, and just by holding them I could feel releases taking place, or they gave me inner confidence. If I was drawn to different stones, then they would help me with whatever I needed it for. It was my body self-selecting the right remedy through crystals.

All the natural gemstones contain minerals from the earth, and just as we gain our essential minerals from our root vegetable from the sources of the earth, the stones work in similar way. Our body can tell us when we are craving certain foods to eat, because we are lacking that mineral that the vegetable can provide. This also works in the same way with the stones from the earth. Each stone will have different metaphysical properties that offer our body strength in some way. The Himalayan salt rocks are made up of all the earth minerals that allow our body to absorb until it's had enough. That's why bathing in natural Himalayan baths salt's is one of the best things you can do for your body.

I felt drawn to look at other options and enrolled on certain courses connected to the body energies and how you can work with it.

I was managing to maintain my friend's health through my new found inner guidance, however, it was hard and several times she had nasty attacks that frightened us.

She struggled with maintaining her energy due to her diet being so limited, I started to research natural food and see what it could do for your body. She went and had a private nutritional assessment, as her bloods showed nothing abnormal from the Doctor's . The nutritional assessment came back with a list of foods she could eat and couldn't eat. The list of foods that she couldn't eat was so limiting her diet became very sparse and repetitive, she soon got tired of eating the same foods. Her mental health was being affected as it was getting her down and she couldn't see a return out of this limited world. As going out for meals wasn't possible, and even just having a light sandwich out would cause her to have a reaction. Her diet was so restricted that she couldn't get enough nutrition from her diet. Her immune system was shot to bits and her body was failing her. It was scary times. The natural gemstones helped as they were natural tools we were working with.

Then I had a eureka moment!

My friend had returned from work and I saw how little life was in her eyes, she had no physical energy left and her body ached and hurt in places. Especially her stomach, her head had that light headed feeling and dizzy, she felt nauseous and sick. She wanted to eat but was too frightened to because it made her feel worse when her body couldn't digest the food.

I realised... "You're being drained; someone is taking your energy!!!!"

I'm sure we have all experienced being around someone that can just drain our energy away from us. You come away feeling like you just want to go to sleep. You subconsciously try and avoid that person when you next see them, as you know they will do it again to you. This is an exchange of energy that is taking place, you are being drained.

It was as if someone was guiding me, but all I wanted to do was send love to the person who had drained her. I felt I needed to counteract the draining effect. So I did just that. I connected just like the Buddha's do when they

How To Find Your Inner Happiness

meditate, as I had been feeling a calling to work this way, and I just asked for love to be sent to the person who had drained her.

Through my own journey I realised the only way to counteract this draining feeling it to treat it with honey and not vinegar. On my courses I had been taught to work with light....but real energy shifts were taking place in the universe and sometimes when I channelled through my chakras (energy zones in our body) it didn't feel right anymore.

I felt drawn and through different signs and meditations I was being shown to work with the LOVE energy.

As through my journey I can feel other peoples energy blocks in my body, just the same as the person who is experiencing the pain. Sometimes it's not pleasant to feel other peoples' pain, so I asked my inner tuition if there was another way to feel a patients energy blocks but not physically feel it. This is what I was shown, and this is the way I still work now.

Within minutes my friend felt her stomach churning, and movement going on in her stomach and bowels, the energy shift was starting to place. I felt a real hard pain in my hand when the connection was taking place and slowly over an hour, my friends colour returned to her skin, she felt less sick and her breathing began to calm down. The pain and blocks that were present in my hand, eased.

When I feel energy blocks in my hand, I am shown via acupressure points, as our feet, hands and ears contain acupressure points that release blocks in our meridian lines (energy lines in our body).

My spiritual journey had started....

Chapter Two

PEOPLES FEAR AND INSECURITIES DRAIN OUR ENERGY

THERE HAVE BEEN so many cases that have gone on in my life since then, where I have received clarification that the same effect has been going on with others.

I will list quite a few, because if just a few of these cases help people relate to what they are going through, then this book will be worth it.

Work environments have a competitive vibe going through the office/establishment. There will always be someone who wants to get one over you or be better than you. It's very rare to have a harmonious feeling between all colleagues. There is always someone who is threatened by a newcomer, or jealous of another person being promoted, or envious of someone doing a better job than what they are doing. This causes the wrong wolf to be fed and foreign energy invades another person's body. People are unaware of what they are doing to others, but this happens.

Foreign energy, fear from others causes you to act on the opposite of what you want.

Especially if several of your colleagues or boss have issues with how you work, it can be very hard to keep a positive attitude and keep an uplifted spirit when you carry a foreign/insincere energy. When situations such as this arise, it's best to find an alternative solution for you. It can affect your health, as you are permanently fighting against a strong will of selfishness that isn't good for you. As the old saying goes, 'birds of a feather flock together'. Like for like will be attracted to each of the individuals and the situation that is coming from an insincere place will increase unless it is cleared.

Not only will the individuals be carrying the change of energy it changes the atmosphere all through the company you will feel the victim.

A healthy balance is all about giving and receiving with an equal share. When you give more than you receive back, it's time to leave this unhealthy situation and embrace future change, that's beneficial to you.

If anybody wants something from you, there should be an exchange, not just take from you. Its all about priming the pump.

Situations that I have been involved in caused the jealousy of others to spiral out of control to the point of no return. Action was taken from a personal point of view rather than the benefit of the company, it was triggered off from other people insecurities, but as I was the victim, you just have to go with the flow and keep the faith that there is something better waiting for you. Unless you clear these low vibrations that your body has absorbed from this experience, you will carry them and attract the same situation into your life again. Lessons will keep repeating themselves, as the saying goes 'same meat, different gravy'.

In my case I had to learn what was happening as it presented itself to me time and time again, until I became aware that the scenario was a lesson that I needed to break through.

We act on peoples' fear whether we choose to or not and by realising what is happening it can help keep you strong to get you through the tough times.

If you become aware of the selfish people around you, it will help as it does seem they are the ones you need to watch out for draining your energy and changing the way you feel about yourself. They are the ones feeding the wrong wolf.

The signs to watch out for when someone is feeding the wrong wolf:

- Talking about themselves
- No consideration for others
- Talking over the top of you
- Manipulating situations, so they do what they want to do
- People taking credit of your work

When we are affected by a controlling/foreign energy, you can almost guarantee these symptoms will kick in:

- Doubting your abilities
- Feeling like you don't want to go into work, or avoiding what makes you happy i.e. any hobbies
- Make mistakes, as your feeling confused
- Anxiety attacks, worried or stress signs
- Never finishing anything
- Mental blocks, you struggle to think logically, or creatively (whatever side of the brain matters to you)

All of the above result in confusion that can lead onto depression.

What do we need to do?

Being so sensitive to energy, I can feel others energies around me and pick up peoples pain, discomforts, emotions and stress. Therefore its vital for me to clear these, otherwise I can carry these energies (that are foreign to my body) and it can cause others around me to react to these energies.

My body will repel these foreign energies, and it can block me physically, unbalance my emotions so I change in my moods, ways and outlook on life. You can guarantee I will get a headache, confusion, bloated stomach, blocks in my bowels/urinary system, skin complaints, and feel irritable (they are just a few signs of other peoples energy that has invaded my own).

When I'm being drained by others, all I want to do is sleep, just vegetate and stay in.

Insincere energy is cold and harsh; when insincere energy invades me I feel the coldness around me and in my chest area (heart chakra). My stomach area gets drained (my solar plexus) and then the bloated feeling and tightness around my pelvis kicks in. On one occasion through low vibrations I did get a nasty head imbalance, symptoms were similar to an inner ear infection, although the Doctor couldn't find anything to suggest this. No diagnosis was found, but the symptoms were very present.

Animals are affected by insincere energies, just the same as we are. With my cat his sinuses become congested and he goes off his food; my horses their bowels aren't as active as they should be and their muscles go tight, they also convert to flight mode. Their behaviour changes and they get a bit bolshy.

Attacks have even occurred when I have been riding or handling my horse. The insincere thought from another left me with a light headedness feeling, my stomach immediately started to get pains and my horse switched to flight mode, put on a grand display of naughtiness and decided to play up. Before the insincere thought process arrived she was calmly grazing. Their have been other occasions when I have been riding; in the school and when one of the other horse owners drove into the yard. My horse switched to flight mode, she stopped listening to my aids, head in the air and on a mission to run everywhere.

You have to see it to believe it sometimes, it is like someone has flicked a switch, and they are a different horse altogether. I realise what is happening, but for people that don't, it can feel like your horse has just had a split personality.

Anyone extremely sensitive, it's easy to absorb energy waves that have been sent to another. I've witnessed on several occasions this happening.

- Someone came down with a urine infection when the insincere thought was sent to me.
- Also another common one is 'hot flush' I remember feeling an insincere energy around me, and another lady who was standing by me, came over in a hot flush. She blamed it on her hormones, but I was aware the change of energy caused this.

Chapter Three

A BIG DOWN FALL IS JEALOUSY

IF SOMEONE IS more popular, jealousy will arise. Negative thoughts will be sent and the receiver will carry contaminated energy. The contaminated energy will now take on an action of its own and put the senders fear into the mix. The receiver will feel different and they will change in their actions, and thoughts. Their passions will not seem so important. This new contamination has taken on a life of its own. The victim will feel different to other people and it will cause them to feel like other people have an issue with them, they will feel isolated.

Hence how an influence change you.

The exchange of contaminated energy is the catalyst of further low vibrations to be drawn to you. As this contamination your carrying can act like a drug and the magnet of attraction just invites you to similar situations/people without you realising.

You can see how so many people who are on this journey to find themselves/soul searching have become consumed by other energies, that their mind is now a cocktail of emotions.

E R Claridge

Other symptoms that arise from carrying contamination:

- Memory loss
- Stomach complaints
- Craving sweet foods
- Body temperature changing
- Feeling lost or trapped in a situation
- Self-doubting yourself and abilities
- Losing confidence
- Irrational mood swings/behaviours
- No passion or excitement for anything
- Lost interest in life
- No drive
- Feel lethargic
- Agree to things for a quiet life
- Changing personality

Other cases...

Long standing friendships can change when someone new comes in to the equation with an insecure energy. The insecure energy causes the victim to start changing in their thought process, the fear they are now carrying starts to take control and the real energy that was them is drained away, like sand through your fingers.

When anyone comes from a place of sincerity there should be no imbalance of energy that one person can change so much or be pushed in a situation to leave anything sincere.

When a contaminated energy exchange takes place you can almost see the force of the energy manipulating another to change. It's sad, but everyone has options, and this is where you can find the right people to fit in your life by keeping clear of contaminated energy.

Case one - My paths crossed with this lady who is a friend now, where she had experienced much of what I am saying. Her previous husband had manipulated her life to his choice of friends she spent time with, a material existence of new gadgets, big house, big holidays and it was all about him. It wasn't until she became seriously ill and a tumour appeared on her back that she really found out how selfish he was, there was no sincerity in his feelings, it was all him and his materialistic world i.e. holidays and new gadgets. It was explained to both of them that she would need recovery time after the treatment, this meant time off work, so the pennies would be tighter than normal. There was no sincerity towards her at all; it was all about what he couldn't have anymore. It was a turning point for her and she finally realised she had to get out before his selfishness caused her further illness.

Case Two - Daisy had a similar situation with a selfish boyfriend that had been manipulating her life. It was all about him, and he was living life as a single man, as if she wasn't in the equation. She started to lose her identify, drive and passion for life. She didn't know who she was anymore. He was cheating on her, even though they were engaged. Her diet wasn't healthy, all she craved was sugary foods, she was losing weight rapidly, and it was turning into a slippery slope for her. Her turning point came when she had a miscarriage and there was no emotion on his part, he seemed relieved. She knew this wasn't what she wanted and it only really hit her, when she went out with friends and she caught him out with another woman. She called it a day and she walked away from it all, this meant walking away from the new house they were having built, the material things they had together. By rights she could have fought him and got what was rightfully hers, however, she was exhausted from him and just wanted to walk away from all of it. She got a new job which relocated her to another county within the UK. It was then she started to rebuild her life again.

Case Three - Mandy couldn't lift her arm; she had pain in her upper arm. When I saw her I got a name and sent that person love, the pain eased in her arm as I was there. She had already been to see the Doctor and taken painkillers this hadn't helped, the insincere energy had started to cause this pain and it was getting worse.

Case Four - On another occasion Mandy experienced shooting pain in between her eyes, she is a smoker and it was happening whenever she went to light her cigarette she got this nasty pain come on. She went to the opticians and there didn't seem to be anything wrong, although the symptoms were very present. So I connected for her, and asked to feel her pain. When I was shown what she was feeling the hazy head, was intense, it felt like the brain couldn't engage or think straight as it felt like a thick fog, I stayed connected until I felt all the fog clear, thankfully so did her symptoms.

Case Five - Mandy's dog struggled with his bowels, he was under the Vets guidance and ended up on steroids, which left him with a high temperature and extremely restless. They couldn't diagnose exactly what was wrong without opening him up. It was believed to be an infection of some description. So Mandy asked me to see what I felt. I connected and felt bloated and a pain in the small intestine area, this was where the vets believed the problem was too. One evening he was off his food and just extremely restless and panting, Mandy asked me to connect so I did. I just stayed connected and asked for the love energy to come through to her dog, to clear him of any other energies he was carrying. After about half an hour, he did the licking and chewing thing, then got up and started to look for food, he ate some of his food, passed wind and then started to pull his toys out to play. He obviously was starting to feel back to himself and his normal behaviour started to return.

Case Six - Johnny was struggling with everything going wrong in his life; whatever way he turned something would happen in a negative way. He was attracting negativity into his life without knowing it. He asked if I could help with his knee injury, he received through playing football. So I connected for him, immediately I got that he was carrying contaminated energy that was blocking him and attracting negativity into his life. So I cleared this, he wasn't too sure what to make of it, but knew something had changed. A week later he thanked me, said he didn't know what I had done but he was feeling more positive and things had changed for the better.

Case Seven - Louise had horrendous tooth pain and was suffering with IBS, I offered to see I could ease it. So I connected when I did I got another energy that was causing this and it turned out to be conflict at work, a power struggle. I cleared the low vibrational energy and the pain eased. I told Louise what I thought had caused it and it appeared that last time a big influential meeting took place; she had toothache around the dates before she was due to fly out to another country to attend the meeting. It did seem this certain persons' energy caused her toothache.

When another person has a negative thought towards you, it has a draining effect on you. The first sign is not only confusion in the mind, but feeling nauseous. Energy is always taken from (solar plexus chakra) the small intestine area, in energy terms is known as the energy vortex, the one that keeps you full of drive and energy.

Chapter Four

WHAT DO YOU FEEL?

WHEN YOU ARE clear of low vibrations you don't have anything in your mind. So if you are one of these people that cannot switch off and your mind is just continuously thinking about the next thing or you can't get someone out of your mind or a situation. Then it is time to clear.

I can say that when I close my eyes and I know I am being drained of my energy. When I connect and clear it feels like I see picture slides just flicking through my head, until they are gone. This I can only assume is other people insecurities that have been erased out of my mind.

When I say connect, I am connecting to the high vibration energy that is much bigger than each of us, the positive energy that is available to all of us from the universe. It's the high vibration that we connect to when we meditate/dream the escape from the negative chains that trap us on this earth.

The universe is one big vortex of energy; it's what holds the world up, the connection to the sun. When there is a high vibration such as the sun, it allows our higher consciousness to connect, it cleanses our minds and leaves

E R Claridge

us feeling free of heavy burdensome troubles, it's a therapy in itself.

When we breathe in fresh air and positive energy, we exhale toxins. To be outdoors feeds us, it's where our soul feels good. Fresh air cleanses our toxins and exercise helps break down toxins so we feel free again. The more in tune you become with how your body feels when it's free of toxins and other people's energy, the more aware you are when you have been intoxicated by others.

When any insincere energy affects us it blocks us, stops us from living the life we should lead, puts fear in us and causes us to act on the opposite of what is right for us.

The insincere energy somehow feeds of us, so we feel drained, lifeless, confused and just feel out of sorts.

The only way to restore balance is to counteract this process.

Chapter Five

HOW DID IT AFFECT ME?

FOR YEARS AND years, I was easily influenced without realising. So many actions and paths that I took wasn't me, yet I still carried on as it was my only option at the time or so my head was telling me.

I would find myself doing things against my own gut instinct, hang out with people that didn't give me confidence, accept people into my life that just made me feel inferior... the list goes on...

I can see now I was carrying so many energies from others, that I wasn't sure who the real me was. I needed to embrace my passions; it's a struggle when you are being controlled by other people energies. Until you feel clear you don't realise you are carrying other energies. Note to self: if you don't feel yourself and feel lost, your carrying contamination.

There are 3 main things that kept me grounded when I was going through this influence stage, and it was those 3 things, that got me through the blocks that I was experiencing. The first was unconditional love from my mother, she was always there for me no matter what, and at the time I didn't realise that she was going through a negative journey herself, she helped me find the positive things in my life. The other was my horses, my passion, I neglected riding them and spending time with them through a stage of my life but mum kept me strong and the horses kept me grounded, they were a way of life and they kept reminding me of who I am and what I love, the third thing was music, I couldn't get enough house, trance, drum and bass music, I realise now this was my own way of cleansing. Music is an essential element to lifting our spirit.

Having lived through this I can say my energy is extremely sensitive to any negative/low vibrations, so anything insincere affects me, through absorbing, insincere thoughts from others, gossip, and being around negative people/selfish people. This is the main reason I have worked with the divine high energy and written this book, is to help others, so they remain true to their own energy.

When we are born I like to think of us as pure clean energy, but as life unfolds for each of us, we all experience negativity. Some more than most, and the pure vessel that is you, is lost.

One evening I got shown through meditation an image and it was a skeleton in a dark cupboard covered by cobwebs with a faint light just flickering. This faint light is the soul of that person that is desperate to be fed with the right energy. When people feed off their energy, it leaves them retracting away from everything that they need to feed this light again. Hence, how depressed people feel happier shutting themselves away. The best thing is to move out of the dark place that is falsely holding you hostage (trapped in fear) and feed your soul.

This was shown to me so I realised how an overpowering energy can affect you.

When we are surrounded by selfish people, they have a strong energy, you can feel or I can feel the coldness that they project, they are cut off from the loving flow of the universe and are only thinking of one self. It attacks the head, and feels like a block is sitting in your thinking process, next you will get a pain somewhere in your body, and it can come on in minutes. This is an outside energy that is overpowering your energy, it's the bigger pebble that creates stronger ripples, and the ripples of this bigger stone overrides your own ripples.

Being around this energy and living with it, drains you, when it drains you, it just feeds off you, until you become that skeleton in the cupboard with a faint light flickering. Your thoughts are scattered, your actions aren't coming from a sincere place. You act on this new energy that is now feeding your consciousness. The passion for life you once felt has gone and material things now become a priority. You start to feed the wrong wolf. Attracting more and more chaos into your life, that is miles from the life you should be living.

It is advised when you are carrying low vibrations to cut the cord. This is how it seems to work; the insincere energy connects a cord from them to you, and then drains your energy out of you. This will continue until you just feel exhausted and the pull of energy will leave you thinking about that person and because they will be exchanging their energy with yours, you will falsely be led to believe that they are good people for you. You will push away all that is sincere in your life and keep attracting more people and situations like this into your life, hence how mid-life crisis comes about and serious mental health conditions arise.

The fear just knocks your confidence and you lose the drive to complete projects or be as passionate about life as you use to be.

I've lost count how many times, I've had to clear myself from other peoples energies, as they would lead me to doubt my abilities in my hobbies, passions and work.

Quite often if I found myself in environments where I was networking and sharing ideas or suggesting positive business development ideas I would suddenly become congested and felt it a struggle to talk.

I know this was a block coming from an outside influence that resented me sharing ideas, or being recognised for my forward thinking, this has also happened at family gatherings. It felt like I wanted to clear my throat all the time, and I do recall being on a night out and it felt like I was coming down with a sore throat. As I was innocent and unaware of the truth, I didn't realise I was collecting all the low vibrations, from one initially that then became the catalyst to attract others.

A common symptom for me is when other peoples energy would consume me is to feel bloated. There was a workplace that really sticks in my mind and I know where the low vibration came from that made me feel like this, and other colleagues also suffered with the same symptoms. Looking back now I can see they definitely came from one person and their insincere thoughts. It certainly had a draining effect on me. They were obsessed with their weight, keeping trim and I would crave sugar like it was going out of fashion, I would often find myself nearly falling asleep at the wheel of the car when driving home, because my energy had been drained out of me. I was unknowingly carrying other energy around and this attracted further energies like the original one, until my mind was a cocktail of mixed and low vibrations that I didn't know if I was coming or going.

At the time I didn't realise how negative feelings were towards me, but looking back I can see ego and greed was running this persons life and it was their own fear/insecurity that projected all of this negativity towards me, that naturally attracts like for like.

When this came to an end, I went and attracted a similar situation into my life, that was like for like. Crazy how it works, but the lessons keep repeating themselves until you cleanse of the low vibrations. (Hence, why I want people to be aware)

I also worked in a very competitive environment in recruitment at one stage, I started at the same time as another girl and the industry was all new to me as it was structured and civil industry in the public sector. It was a great opportunity for anyone who was hungry for recognition and cut throat business. I was put in a team, and didn't receive much help at all, while the other girl who started received plenty of help. Any way I cracked on with the job in hand and I managed to get one applicant lined up for the job pretty much straight away, the feeling I felt afterwards was mixed it was happiness, but the coldness and uncertainty I also felt was overpowering, I now realise this was my colleague who also wanted the same applicant for a job in the private sector. His fear was causing me to feel confusion over my job, and not long after this I quit as my mind was a cocktail of emotions and I couldn't handle going into work anymore. This is just one example of how cut throat sales business can be, and if you're sensitive like me, it really does have a devastating effect on you.

Chapter Six

ANOTHER CASE

SALLY EXPERIENCED NEGATIVITY in her life at a very early age, and this just attracted more and more people that contained the same negative energy into her life. By the time she was into her 50's her body had just cried out enough is enough. At the pinnacle of these events and through my own spiritual journey I was able to see what was happening and cleansed all the negative energies that her body had absorbed to get some normality back into her life.

Her way of dealing with life was to throw herself into her work, it was her only time to be on her own and keep her sane. She went from a controlled upbringing as a child to another in her marriage, both parties were extremely selfish. The power of her mind just told her to keep going and she ignored all her bodies symptoms that were starting to show, until they actually stopped her from working at the level she was. She sought her own way to gain release, which helped her immensely through the grey years, but because she had been attracting it into her life from such an early age and some of it was blood related, it was impossible to completely dispose of everything in her life. But in her own time, she is dealing with cleansing away all the people as and when opportunities present themselves. In the meantime she is keeping clear of the negative energy that comes her way, through connecting and carrying tools such as gemstone crystals that she wears in jewellery form.

This brings me onto lessons, I think so many of us find ourselves in situations where we get the same scenario presented to us time and time again. This will keep repeating itself until you realise what is happening and how to clear it.

Only then will the right things start to come into your life and only then will your true divine guidance be shown to you so you can obtain what you actually want in life, not what another energy is telling you.

There are so many incidences in people's life where they feel uncomfortable around people, inferior, forget things, have a memory loss, or might say something completely stupid and you can't think for the life of you why you said this. This will be other people's energy contaminating/controlling you.

I can reel off so many cases that other people have experienced, but it all boils down to one thing, when they are being controlled by a low vibration, health symptoms will arise, their actions will change, their outlook will change and their personality will change.

We are not made to carry other peoples energy, our body is made complete with our own energy, so we just need to read the signs when we are not clear and do something about it.

Chapter Seven

WHAT IS AN INTENTION AND INFLUENCE?

THE OXFORD DICTIONARY says an intention is 'having the attention applied, an aim or purpose'. The aim of a negative intention is to work it to that person's advantage.

Influence – the capacity to have an effect on the character, development, or behaviour of someone or something, or the effect itself.

So this is what happens the intent behind someone with a negative mind set, can influence you to behave differently, change to the person you truly are, and encourages you to adopt new hobbies and drop off old friend to bring in new friends.

What effect does this have on you?

Health issues, depression, stress, you adopt a negative mind set, and lack of self esteem etc.

All of these conditions don't come on over night, they gradually build up, and you will find yourself unhappy, starting to look at life with the glass half empty, be really tired, because you are carrying round these intentions, you're not free to express who you want to be. Draining energy, I call them energy vampires. You can be standing next to someone or in someone's company and the next minute you find yourself exhausted, you feel shattered and just want to sleep. This is a pure example of your energy being drained from you. You feel mentally and physically exhausted.

Depending what the intention is it can find you being blocked from the things that are right for you. Example; if you find yourself out of work and you know you are skilled and capable, an intention can block any jobs from coming your way or more to the point a job that is right for you. This is turn can affect your self-esteem and you start underestimating yourself. Work colleagues are very renowned for being competitive, and they have to be better than you, it's natural to always compare to someone who is in the same line of work with you. Where you might feel that is great their doing well. The other party might be very competitive in their mind set, and their intention would be strong, willing themselves to do better than you, and in turn this would knock your self-confidence, by causing contamination in you and you start to doubt your abilities etc.

Children getting in with the wrong crowd, they become influenced and change towards their parents; they tend to shut themselves off from their peers, and adopt new activities and friends. Depending on the influence they can change any way and in turn lose their passion as to what they want for themselves. They have someone else's energy in them that is influencing their mind and their decisions they choose to make. I recently came across someone's daughter who was influenced to stop her passion, and take on all different subjects for her A levels, as her friends were doing the courses. Only to find herself lost and wanting to go back to her passion, and go to College instead. It is scary how an influence can change us so much.

Animals are really quick at picking up peoples intentions. I have horses myself and I find it fascinating how quickly they feel an intention come their way. It's like watching a light switch, you just see them change into the flight mode and switch off from partnership when you're riding or walking in hand. The amount of intentions I have had to clear from my horses, just to get them back to their normal self. This again can affect them mentally and health wise.

Relationships are an interesting one; they say you know if you are attracted to someone in 20 seconds. I see time and time again, people change to fit in with another person's lifestyle, they say it's working together (compromise) but what I see is one partner dominating (influencing) the other so they change their lifestyle to fit in with them. This could mean dropping off their own hobbies, friends (because the dominating partner doesn't' like the influence their friends have on them), their outlook changes, they can become very harsh towards ones they love, and start to resent their life. A lot of the time one partner can manipulate the other, and start knocking them down mentally. It can become a vicious circle and their self-esteem goes so low, that they slip into depression, start to lose interest in their passion; something they are good at, they feel like they just need to get through each day, go on auto mode and feel numb and lose the passion for life and what it's all about.

The victim of the party doesn't see the changes that are taking place, just feel low and exhausted all the time, they lose their confidence and start to shut themselves away. Sometimes serious depression can kick in and they end up on pharmaceutical drugs just to get them through each day.

This type of behaviour will be coming from an insincere heart, someone with a hidden agenda that will be a benefit to them.

It takes all sorts to make up this world. But from my experience the people you need to watch out for are the selfish ones they have a hard exterior and will stop at nothing to get where they want to be. Their needs become so big and they are so shut off from other people's feelings, that as far as they are concerned life owes them, and they will have what they want! These sorts of people don't see the pebble effect in the water they have created, and how people's life has had to change to fit in with them. Certainly their negative minds set, can influence people around them to think differently, change in their personality, change towards close friends and take on new approaches to handle people.

The health issues will kick in with the victim, as the contamination will be having a destructive pattern on the

How To Find Your Inner Happiness

victim's brain and body, it will be overriding the normal functions and messages of the body, the body will start to rebel and neuron activity (see chapter on the brain) will take on a destructive pattern to the body.

This is how mid-life crisis comes about, suddenly people have enough of what they have in life and feel the need to embrace things they never did earlier on in life that they wanted to. They rebel and need to express themselves the way they want to.

Our bodies are not made for contaminations to control us.

People who hit fame quickly have a tough ride, because I can only imagine how many intentions they receive, but in turn this can affect their talent, their confidence etc. I can see why so many people need a release like alcohol, drugs or keeping fit. The latter is the best way to go in many ways, however, not everyone does. It can be a sad and lonely existence for those that feel they are popular because of their fame. They do need to be aware how intentions can influence their mind set.

John Lennon had the right idea, peace and love. With the mindset of love, there is no negativity, this is definitely the way forward, and people won't need to go soul searching because we will be in tune with our intuition and gut feelings. We will be adopting the right lifestyle and attracting the right people into our life.

Changing the thought to LOVE in our mind is the way forward.

Chapter Eight

SO WHAT'S IT ALL ABOUT HOW DO WE GET IN THIS MENTALLY CONFUSED STATE?

Our body's energy run on equivalent to an electric circuit and when another current of electric interferes it changes the flow of our life and goals.

The trick is to keep your electrical current free of contamination like the water keeping it pure, but with the greed of today and people feeding off it this is getting harder to do.

So we need a way to be free from this to follow our dreams without contamination and enjoy life with the right people and right balance.

Due to the universal shifts i.e. the planets lining up we have experienced many disturbances of imbalance in the earth hence all the natural disasters, we have been slowly awakening to helping the planet and ourselves but mixed messages have come forward and really unsettled minds and disturbances have caused tragic losses and sadness during this time.

Just like us the earth is only a part in all the universal being. The earth has chakras just like we do and if they get blocked the same as ours then the flow isn't a happy one and something has to give. That's why the love energy is a much greater power/force than ever you or I can imagine and by asking for the intention of love to clear away the blocks it can result in a happier existence.

The 7 chakras on Earth (Coon, 2012)

Number	Chakra Locations
1	Mt Shasta, California, USA – The Root Chakra
2	Lake Titicaca, Peru-Bolivia, South America – The Sacral Chakra
3	Uluru-Kata Tjuta, Northern Territory, Australia – The Solar Plexus Chakra
4	Glastonbury and Shaftesbury, England – The Heart Chakra
5	Great Pyramid, Mt. Sinai, Mt of Olives, Middle East – The Throat Chakra
6	Aeon activation chakra, mobile (currently stationary) – The Third Eye Chakra
7	Mount Kailas, Tibet – The Crown Chakra

Chakras play an important part to understanding our own energy zones and how they work.

Chakra means wheel or vortex of energy, and it refers to the 7 energy zones of our consciousness. The chakras are also connected to each endocrine gland (the function of the endocrine system balances the hormones)

The Crown Chakra – Violet - located at the top of the head – spiritual connection, higher consciousness, understanding, oneness – pineal gland

The Third Eye Chakra – Indigo - located between your eyebrows – psychic abilities, clairvoyance, inner knowing – pituitary gland

The Throat Chakra – Blue - in the throat area – communication, speech, self expression – thyroid gland

The Heart Chakra – Green- in the heart/lungs area – love, balance, compassion – thymus gland

The Solar Plexus Chakra – Yellow – in the small intestine area – power, control, willpower – pancreas gland

The Sacral Chakra – Orange – in the large intestine area – creativity, drive, sexual energy, ambition – the adrenal glands

The Root Chakra – Red – instinct, survival, finances, security – ovaries or gonads

The previous ancestors have had historical buildings built to help us with clearing our chakras and especially with the Egyptians, drawings and sketches have been emphasised on buildings for us never to forget our cleansing rituals to keep the earth in a healthy existence. (Mark,2009)

Chapter Nine

WHAT IS ENERGY AND HOW DOES IT AFFECT US?

SUNLIGHT IS OUR main source and provider of light, heat and energy. Not only does the sunlight sustain all life on earth, but it also sustains the Earth itself. It provides plants with the energy of photosynthesis, which in turn sustains the lives of all animals and humans.

Without the sun we would not exist or the earth.

We always feel good when the sun is out, because it is cleansing away low vibrations, it's like a detox to our body. However, it is important as with drugs to get the right amount and not over do it.

There have been so many planetary shifts that the magnetic field around the earth is going through adjustments and we are seeing the outcome through natural disasters.

Just like the earth has its own magnetic field (British Geological Survey), we also have our own magnetic energies, and when shifts like this take place universally our body picks up on it.

The planetary shifts that have taken place are affecting all of us. We all express it in different ways. The low vibrations that have come from the planetary shifts will be attracted to other low vibrations in the universe/on earth including people that give off low vibrations.

The people that give out low vibrations can do so in a number of ways, through outside influences.

Chapter Ten

HOW DO OUTSIDE INFLUENCES CHANGE OUR ENERGY?

(Emoto, 2001)

DR. M. EMOTO has evidence to prove that positive words can change the frequency in water to a higher vibration, and as our body consists of 70% of water, this would operate in the same way.

Evidence proves that the vibration of water recognises words, and this doesn't need to be spoken aloud, it can be written down.

The positive words like love, give, passion etc raised the vibration as all these words are coming from a place of sincerity, and the photographs show water that has formed beautiful clear snowflakes. Whereas negative words like hate, do it, etc just destruct the water, and leave a heavy colour.

Negative words, generate the senders fear in you, the energy change takes place in the water in your body and the fear keeps you away from what's right for you and you become their puppet. The fear pulls all the strings.

Negative energy has generated a thought process and negative words have been put against your name at some point, this can be a thought, you have been the subject of negative gossip (including personal opinions) or you have been around someone that has a draining, negative effect on you.

If you think about it you know how you feel when you are around someone that always looks at the glass half empty, they just seem to have a pessimistic view on life and you always come away feeling drained. You subconsciously choose to avoid spending time with them as it seems to leave you feeling depressed and not in a good place. Proof that negative words change the water vibration in your body.

This is the same process when someone thinks about you in a negative way, or you are the subject of a conversation and the people are coming across in an insincere way about you, it will affect your energy/vibration without you realising (unless you are extremely sensitive). The people are usually coming from a place of envy, or jealousy, but never the less this doesn't help the victim.

You can always sense a bad atmosphere like when you have just walked into an argument, or a building that has experienced unhappy times. It would be the negativity that you are picking up on. You can absorb this energy and will carry it round with you, just the same as if that person had been there.

This can also work is a positive way, if you think about when the Olympics were held in London, all of the competitors said the crowd were amazing and you could feel the positive energy come from their support towards them. This encouraged the competitors to do well, as there was so much love projecting toward them.

We all realise that these effects take place but don't know how to keep the balance and always keep us true to ourselves.

It seems that words have the power to build us or destroy us.

Chapter Eleven

HOW DOES GOSSIP AFFECT OUR VIBRATIONS?

AS HARMLESS AS you think it is, it isn't!

Gossip contains a low vibration, so any words that are coming from a place of insincerity usually jealousy, resentment related, will have a low vibrational affect on the person/victim in question (Emoto, 2004).

These low vibration affects on the victim will cause them to act off the fear that is coming from an outside influence, and they will not take the right paths that are destined for them. They will be drawn to attract the low vibrational path, from the fear that is controlling them. 'The Law of Attraction'.

A lot of us get hot right or left ears, and people often joke someone is talking about you. All of our acupressure points can be found in our ears (Nogier). So as the low vibrations attack and blocks occur there is a high possibility that the gossip is affecting our ears to itch and become hot.

Health issues will follow suit when the low vibration affects the energy, electrical imbalance in our bodies will occur connected to our neurotransmitters.

The low vibrations will always attack your weak areas, so everyone is different, but you can normally guarantee any breaks, weakening of tendons, ligaments will be one of the first to go, followed by many common deficiencies of the pituitary gland, as the pituitary gland is our intuition antennae that picks up the low vibrations and this is how they filter through, (third eye).

Many other traditions actually wear high vibrational stones around the third eye area (the space in-between your eyes), to help protect this area from any negative outside influences. Others include clearing and grounding the negativity in their head, in a form of prayer.

Bullying

We have evidence to prove the messages we receive, through thought, written or spoken had a lowering vibration on energy. (Emoto, 2004)

So imagine what is happening to the bodies energy, when a bullying process is going on through written social media, texts, verbal, and being around this person who would think this process. Although the bully or bullies will have their own insecurities without realising it, that could have been caused from a trigger point in their childhood, this would have a devastating effect on the victim.

So by recognising the power of words and how it can change your vibrations the victim could start to lift out of this devastating effect.

Bullying can happen anywhere and emotional bullying can be the worst at times. This doesn't need to be someone in school, this can be workplace amongst colleagues or any group or family/friends.

You just need that one person who can come into a situation taking a dislike to someone (the bad apple), and their negative points of view will cause the victim to feel very insecure and change their thought process.

It has been recognised that water is a transporter of energy in our body and as our body is made up of 70% of water, this is now showing that negative words change our vibration in our bodies through our water. (Emoto, 2004)

The earth is mainly made up of water, so anywhere where low vibrations are present this would attract like for like. It draws the low vibrations to it like a magnet and cause disruptions in the earth just as it has done.

So how does this affect us when we hear these words?

As we are all vibrations and evidence has proven that the water changes according to the vibration of the words that are sent our way. This would have the same affect to our water in our body, so the vibration that is in our body could be operating on a high, and then we are surrounded by low morale or people with negative views; this would lower our vibrations and change the activity in the water.

Music raises the vibration of water. Music has been found to be a great remedy for autistic children and can immediately raise the vibration when you are feeling down.

Chapter Twelve

THE POWER OF MUSIC

EVIDENCE HAS PROVEN that music affects the vibration in the water (Emoto, 2004). Further studies are going on that are showing that music can affect the brain and help conditions connected to the brain.

Such as

- Alzheimas disease
- Autism
- Post-traumatic stress disorder
- Dementia
- Stroke
- NICU infants
- Language acquisition
- Dyslexia
- Pain management
- Stress and anxiety
- Coma and more.

Music releases any built up tension, brings out self-expression, enjoyment and allows the mind to wander, bring back memories, encourage emotions from those memories....it is a very powerful energy

Studies are showing that music stimulates both halves of the brain, therefore affecting children when they are growing. By activating both sides of the brain, this will help a child overall cognitive development (Hemley)

Music is one of the very few activities that stimulates both parts of the brain, and in my eyes encouraging it is essential to our life.

How does it work?

The left side of the brain is the logic side – when the music is played the brain can show stronger analytical traits, i.e. process data. This side focuses on the notes and the musical factors.

The right side of the brain is the creative side – where images, ideas and visions come from. This part of the brain focuses on the melody of the music.

By combining the two parts of the brain, the bigger picture is used. However, if we don't activate both parts of the brain, part of the process of decision making can be limited, because you are only seeing it from a factual point (left brain), or opposite to this is the dream type vision etc., i.e. you can picture what you want but don't have the logic sense to see the strengths and weaknesses to achieve this.

There are other activities that also use both parts of the brain, leisure activities such as walking; riding and martial arts will affect them when you're in a steady rhythm (Manjul)

I remember seeing a documentary where there were people who were over 60 years of age walking round a hall to music, they were encouraged to stretch their arm, and move freely to the melody of the music. Reviews after this session, was a general well-being, they felt better in themselves, and had more energy to do more.

Activities involving music will enhance the brain activity in both halves, such as singing, playing an instrument, dancing and working out to music. This will encourage long term benefits as by activating the right side of the brain, the calmness of allowing your free spirit to roam will give you a release feeling and switch off from the mundane duties. Music allows yourself to dream and escape from the logic side for a while.

There has been research to show that musicians that have had long term commitments to music or engage in vocal performance have shown better health in their language skills and memory (Moreno)

Chapter Thirteen

THE BRAIN

THE BRAIN IS responsible for everything that allows our body to connect and function, including the function of the meridian lines (energy lines) running through our body. The brain houses the 2 endocrine glands, the pineal and the pituitary where I am finding the pituitary gland has a lot of involvement with outside influences.

Each of these glands are part of the endocrine system and have their own functions to help our body connect and stay balanced, and without these balanced, we don't feel well in ourselves, mentally or physically.

We are all connected through anatomy and energy lines. This allows us all to function. The most recognised traditional method to clear the energy lines/ meridian lines is through acupuncture. So the western ways are recognising that the energy lines exist, we just haven't embraced the higher shift of consciousness and how this affects our energy lines as well.

E R Claridge

We are just like electric circuits

Our brain has a similar networks to man-made electrical circuits in that it contain elements (neurons) connected by biological waves (nerve fibres). These do not form simple one-to-one electrical circuits like many-man-made circuits, however. Typically neurons connect to at least a thousand other neurons. These highly specialised circuits make up systems with are the basis of perception, action and higher cognitive function.

We must remember years ago when someone was depressed or not quite balanced in the brain, the medical specialist performed electric shocks to the patient, on the brain. This was because the activity in the neuron would change when the electricity entered and activated the neuron.

Its the same when we have our mobile phone too close to another phone there is interference on waves of energy, this is how the human brain to human brain affects another.

Our neurons are sensitive and pick up the vibrations that the earth is going through, also other people's waves. So if someone is thinking of you in an insincere way through their own emotions, our sensitive neurons will absorb this as the energy comes into our own. This will cause our neurons to react to this new energy and can either block or change activity; this in turn affects our bodies and our mind.

Chapter Fourteen

ELECTRICAL IMPULSES ON THE BRAIN

OTHER THAN ELECTRICAL currents and pharmaceutical drugs by mouth, there has been no real proof of how this can be changed.

It has been noted that the neurons are not as active as they use to be and this is causing mental health issues.

New research has found a technique that has claimed to change the brain activity by clipping the ears with a tool that sends through a milder electrical current that helps change the neuron activity and is claiming to deal with depression, insomnia, anxiety, increased heart rate and other symptoms that drugs struggle to do without side effects. (Alpha wave machine)

Waveform technology has been recognised by Alpha stim founded by Dr Kirsch, using Alpha-stim has claimed to relieve depression, insomnia, pain, and anxiety. This is claimed to work by producing healing effects by activating key nerve centres at the brainstem. He studied the neuroendocrine mechanisms of acupuncture and electroacupuncture with Edmund Chen.

The results and reviews are all positive; from my own journey we can all change the low vibrations that are present in us, by connecting to the high vibration, changing a negative into a positive. The neuron activity can be changed by connecting to the high vibration through a technique we can all do.

Another interesting article I came across. An experiment was carried out at the University in Zurich *(*Article in Understanding Depression*) (L. Sinpetru, 2013)*

In order to identify the mechanisms that make people act in a certain way in various social contexts, the scientists carried out a series of experiments with the help of 63 volunteers.

More precisely, they gave each of the individuals a fixed sum of money, and asked them to decide whether or not they wished to share it with an anonymous partner.

Those who agreed to share also had to decide exactly how much money they were ready and willing to part with.

Apparently, the correct thing to do in this situation was to equally split the money with the anonymous partner. Needless to say, doing so went against each of the volunteers' instinct to put their self-interest first.

The researchers later repeated the experiment, only that this time they told the volunteers that they would be punished if they did not do the right thing,

During both these experiments, the scientists used mild electric shocks to up or reduce the levels of neural activity in the volunteers' right lateral prefrontal cortex, i.e. an area at the front of the brain.

"When neural activity in this part of the brain was increased via stimulation, the participants' followed the fairness norm more strongly when sanctions were threatened, but their voluntary norm compliance in the absence of possible punishments decreased," the researchers explain on the official website for the University of Zurich.

"Conversely, when the scientists decreased neural activity, participants followed the fairness norm more strongly on a voluntary basis, but complied less with the norm when sanctions were threatened," they further comment on their findings.

Interestingly enough, the electric shocks they received did not influence the volunteers' understanding of what the right thing to do was. Thus, the zapping merely influenced their behaviour.

....

Hasten to add this would be how another energy invading your own would work in a similar pattern.

Chapter Fifteen

NEUROTRANSMITTERS

NEUROTRANSMITTERS - RELAY messages from neuron to neuron.

This is what I perceive to be happening, when we are being drained of energy, the activity in our neurons are changing. The list below shows the type of neuron and what its function is. When our head is full of other energies, I believe this does have an effect on the activity of our neurons and causes their function to change, sometimes shut off.

I have witnessed a large number of people that suffer from memory loss when they are being drained from their own energy.

<u>How do neurotransmitters affect our body (Neurogistics, 2015)</u>

- Acetylcholine enhances memory and is involved in learning and recall.
- Serotonin helps regulate sleep, appetite, and mood and inhibits pain. Research supports the idea that some depressed people have reduced serotonin transmission. Low levels of a serotonin

How To Find Your Inner Happiness

by product have been linked to a higher risk for suicide.
- Norepinephrine constricts blood vessels, raising blood pressure. It may trigger anxiety and be involved in some types of depression. It also seems to help determine motivation and reward.
- Dopamine is essential to movement. It also influences motivation and plays a role in how a person perceives reality. Problems in dopamine transmission have been associated with psychosis, a severe form of distorted thinking characterized by hallucinations or delusions. It's also involved in the brain's reward system, so it is thought to play a role in substance abuse.
- Glutamate is a small molecule believed to act as an excitatory neurotransmitter and to play a role in bipolar disorder and schizophrenia. Lithium carbonate, a well-known mood stabilizer used to treat bipolar disorder, helps prevent damage to neurons in the brains of rats exposed to high levels of glutamate. Other animal research suggests that lithium might stabilize glutamate reuptake, a mechanism that may explain how the drug smooths out the highs of mania and the lows of depression in the long term.
- Gamma-aminobutyric acid (GABA) is an amino acid that researchers believe acts as an inhibitory neurotransmitter. It is thought to help quell anxiety.
- Epinephrine is an excitatory neurostranmitter is reflective of stress. This neurotransmitter will

> often be elevated when ADHD like symptoms are present and also regulates hear rate and blood pressure

When any electrical current pulsates through the brain, it re activates inactive neurons as this is where the electrical energy source is.

We all live on the earth that has a magnetic field, so changes to the earth/universe will affect us. Hence why some people are sensitive to the full moon and how great we feel when the sun is out. So when another person drains our energy and they somehow take our energy and get stronger by gaining yours, this change of energy will have a knock effect onto the neurons.

This is why I believe so many people are struggling with mental health, because the cycle of greed is growing and the knock on effect to sensitive people, will affect their neuron activity

There has been further evidence that scientist are now experimenting with magnetic rays to change peoples opinions (Dr Colin Holbrook University of California) (A,Keeley,2015), this is very dangerous, as it is messing with peoples free will, but it will work as this is how we influence one another.

Chapter Sixteen

PINEAL GLAND

WHEN WE TAKE a shower, we often receive inspiration or suddenly think of a new idea, this is down to the sensation of the neurotransmitter 'dopamine' being released. Dopamine allows the well being and relaxed feeling to come over us so we can receive message from the right hemisphere, we forget all our worries and just enjoy the sensation of the water running over us.

When we adopt the Buddha hand positions to clear out brain, the same process happens it activates the pineal gland and cleanses any blocks that may be present in the pineal gland and surrounding area (crown chakra – know as the connection to the higher vibration 'the universe').

The pineal gland is responsible for certain neurotransmitters to release chemicals which affect the modulation of sleep patterns.

I feel that the pineal gland keeps the balance (homeostasis) of the body; it regulates the body temperature, and keeps you connected to the high vibration, so your gut instinct can kick in when there is any cause of concern.

Pituitary Gland

The home of the inner knowing is the (third eye chakra) the pituitary, this seems to be the centre point for any low vibrations to penetrate through. Once the low vibrations hit this area, the health in our eyesight, head, memory, immune system, urinary system, stomach complaints and reproductive system seems to become laboured. Increased headaches are likely, as this is affecting the pineal gland, this will be connected to blocking the endocrine system.

If you look up deficiencies of the pituitary gland, you will see that how low vibrations affect us, they mirror the deficiencies found in the pituitary gland.

Chapter Seventeen

MENTAL HEALTH

MENTAL HEALTH TODAY is huge, and nobody knows why so many people are suffering from this condition.

People that have gone through depression and describe how they feel. They all say it's like a black cloud that engulfs their life, they switch off from normality and find everything too much to cope with, sleep is their only answer as they can't face getting up each day and going out in the big world. In my opinion what I have felt when low vibrations have attacked me and others that I have cleared, all mirror these feeling. In severe cases of carrying other people's energies in you, you would have a mixed cocktail of emotions going on in your body, and the thoughts in your head, would be everywhere. It's a job to think logical, your actions aren't coming clearly and you feel like the world is against you.

I clear daily to avoid this engulfing me and running my life, however, it seems that people are carrying this around with them for a lot longer and go through very sad experiences until they get through this, if they do.

People in the public eye are going to receive more resentful thoughts and energies than the average person, when they are carrying around other people's insecurities they feel even more pressure to deliver results that adds to their addictions to drown this horrible feeling out and take it away.

When a foreign energy is changing the electrical activity in our brain and body, we can no longer recognise or fight to continue to be clear headed and be the true person we are destined to be.

We do need to be clear headed to live a healthy and happy existence. This is what all the victims who are going through this must realise that all these feelings and hang ups they have with themselves are false and the only reason they are feeling this is due to another person's resentment, jealousy etc. The person is experiencing false entrapment.

The more creative and sensitive person you are the more vulnerable and open you are to carrying other peoples stronger energies in you, it will overpower your own. For an example a managers, or team leader, will want to get the maximum out of you, ride on your talents if you like. They don't realise the hidden pressure that they will be putting in you, by coming from an insincere place, (they are feeding the wrong wolf), you will end up carrying this overpowering energy, and will take actions based on this, that could cause you blocks, and result in ill health mental and physical.

All the patterns of a depressed person will start to echo that other persons insecurities; especially at school, if another pupil is jealous of another capabilities they feed off the victim, till the victim doesn't know what they are doing or lose interest in learning, feel tired, can't be bothered and lose confidence in going out and socialising. All because another student is jealous of how popular they are or how intelligent they are.

CHAPTER EIGHTEEN

HIGH VIBRATION

WHAT DO I mean by the high vibration?

The only way I can explain it is a calm energy, that is available to all. The stress of life fades away it's like a wave of positivity that takes over.

It lifts away any heaviness that is dragging you down.

So when the love energy is around the vibrations that ripple through the body are so uplifting.

Most people find this energy when they meditate, having the faith and connecting to a high vibration clears the mind. When you are connecting to hope, the law of attraction works with the thought process and attracts the right energy to work through you.

The energy I work with is 'love' so anything that is connected to love works through me when I connect.

When I connect I'm connecting to the love vibration, and for each person animal I connect to, I immediately feel any blocks present in the mind and body that are not connected to love, this is how the energy clearing treatments take place.

The connection acts like a radar that homes into anything that shouldn't be present.

The cases in the book are just a few examples that can happen when the thought process is not coming from a loving space.

The only way to clear these blocks others have caused us, is to counteract it with the opposite energy.

Each and everyone has the ability to do this and without technology like the alpha wave machine. It just choosing to embrace that the high vibration does exist and working with it.

The more sensitive you are the quicker you will feel it, it's just time that will allow the sensitivity to get stronger so blocks that are holding you back can be felt.

Chapter Nineteen

THE SIGNS

HOW DO YOU know when you are on the right path?

The high vibration shows us lovely signs in many ways when you are on the right path, or something is right for you.

The first is a feather – delicate white feathers that fall in your path, this is a sign to let you know that loved ones are around and guiding you. The sign of a white feather confirms you are on the right path.

How To Find Your Inner Happiness

The Clouds – the sky talks to you, the clouds form wonderful shapes to show you, your being watched over, and the world is made up of something far bigger that guides us, then we know.

The colours in the sky – I often see blobs of rainbow that appear from no-where, no rainbow is present but a lovely splodge of rainbow just appears.

The Robin – a robin will appear whenever a loved one who has passed is near. They appear and watch over you.

How To Find Your Inner Happiness

Magpies – the magpies warn me, if the one magpie appears, I know that bad energy has been sent my way, through thought, or words, or the day isn't going to go so well. So whenever, I see the one, I ask the 'Angels to resolve it' and usually two appear later on down the road; I remember when I was seeking advice on something someone had told me, my gut instinct was telling me it wasn't for me, and the one magpie was about, as soon as I went back to what I know, two flew by.

Technology – energy loves connecting through electrics, so any name, song, place etc that sticks in your mind, and confirms that its more than just a coincidence is evidence that your are being guided. Quite often the T.V will flick to let me know loved ones are around, or my phone will randomly show someones name, just confirming that this person is thinking about me, whether it be in a negative way or loved way, its confirmation they are helping you.

E R Claridge

Never think of yourself on your own, if you ask the love energy to guide you, and to block that is not right for you, it will. All you have to do is ask for love energy to come forward.

Chapter Twenty

THE CONCLUSION

THE CONCLUSION, IS the way the neurons work in your brain, they can be over ridden by a stronger current, i.e. influence, energy that someone is carrying, or you can absorb it.

There are two key areas this takes place, your stomach (solar plexus area) and the head (third eye and crown chakra). These areas start to show unhealthy symptoms such as bloated feeling, or headaches.

The more sensitive you are the stronger you feel it. It is a conflict fighting with your own energy.

The sins of life cause conflicts in people, when a person thinks of someone in an insincere way, the more conflicts we inflict on someone.

The sins of life are feeding the wrong wolf…. This ends in unhappiness.

LOVE is the only energy that can undo all this pain and hurt that are being bottled up, to result in this greed growing. You will find most people that are carrying these conflicts will withdraw from what is right for them, and

E R Claridge

embrace the energy the conflict has instilled in them. Also it doesn't end there, as the law of attraction will attract other energies like the new conflict that each individual is carrying. This results in a lonely world as the conflict energy is now controlling your head over what you want, instead of your own free will and the actions with the conflict in the conscious mind, will have different actions to someone who has a clear mind.

So the tip to change this is a mixture of LOVE and connecting using the Buddha technique to work with the positive energy in the universe.

Diagram below shows you how to connect.

Connect both hands in this way, the left receives and the right gives.

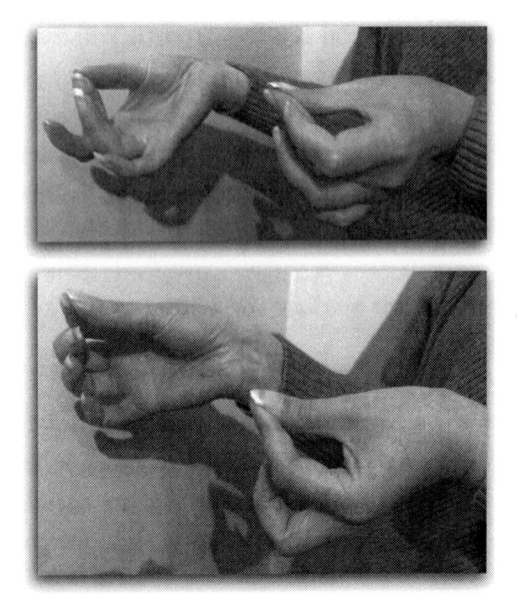

It's important to protect yourself when connecting, so I follow this routine:

1. First ask for the love energy to ground you
2. Then ask for the love energy to bring your guides through
3. Next ask your guides to ground you and protect you
4. I then ask 'Archangel Michael' to cut any cords that are in me
5. Then in your head ask for the following affirmation that you feel is right for you 'love can you cleanse my energy' or 'love to the owners of the energy that is in me' or 'love can you correct what is wrong with me' and 'love to conflicting energies in me'.

Stay connected until you feel better, and the symptoms are starting to disappear, or do this for 20-30 mins each day.

You will start to feel the energy and movement will take place in your stomach area, and also changes will take place in the head, correcting the imbalance. You will feel lighter and your mind will clear.

You can also do this for buildings, stables, yards etc

Once you have finished you need to protect yourself again. Say thank you and then follow through the next 3 steps.

Go through the same routine as above:

1. First ask for the love energy to ground you
2. Then ask for the love energy to bring your guides through
3. Next ask your guides to ground you and protect you

The more sensitive you are the more the quicker you will feel the blocks moving, however, keep at it and you will start to sensitise yourself to the connection.

REFERENCES

R.Coon (2012) Earth Chakras http://earthchakras.org/Locations.php

M. Emoto (2004) Of What Is the Universe Made pg 5 – 28. The Hidden Messages in Water

Dr. Kirsch, (accessed 2016) Alpha stim. The Clinical History of the Alpha – Stim...Waveform technology

L. Sinpetru (2013) Researchers pin down area of the brain that compels people to obey social norms. University of Zurich

Neurogistics (accessed 2015) What are neurotransmitters?

BIBLIOGRAPHY

R.Coon (2012) Earth Chakras http://earthchakras.org/Locations.php

J. Mark (2009) Temple (Ancient History) http://www.ancient.eu/temple/

The Earths Magnetic Field : An Overview. British Geological Survery (accessed 2016)

M. Emoto (2004) Of What Is the Universe Made pg 5 – 28. The Hidden Messages in Water

P.Nogier (accessed 2016) What is Auricular Acupuncture. http://sedatelec.com/english/acupauri.htm

A. Novotney (2013) Music as a Medicine. American Psychological Association

A. Hemley (2000) How does music stimulate left and right brain function. Why is this important?

E. Glenn Schellenberg, University of Toronto (2005) Music and cognitive abilities. Current directions in Psychological Science.

Dr. Kirsch, (accessed 2016) Alpha stim. The Clinical History of the Alpha – Stim…Waveform technology

Neurogistics (accessed 2015) What are neurotransmitters?

L. Sinpetru (2013) Researchers pin down area of the brain that compels people to obey social norms. University of Zurich

A. Keeley (2015) Research that is simply beyond belief. University of Zurich